The Technology of Farming

Producing Fruits

Lori McManus

www.raintreepublishers.co.uk
Visit our website to find out more information about Raintree books.

To order:
☎ Phone 0845 6044371
🖹 Fax +44 (0) 1865 312263
🖳 Email myorders@raintreepublishers.co.uk

Customers from outside the UK please telephone +44 1865 312262

Raintree is an imprint of Capstone Global Library Limited, a company incorporated in England and Wales having its registered office at 7 Pilgrim Street, London, EC4V 6LB – Registered company number: 6695582

Edited by Abby Colich, Megan Cotugno, and Nancy Dickmann
Designed by Victoria Allen
Picture research by Elizabeth Alexander
Illustrations by Oxford Designers & Illustrators
Originated by Capstone Global Library Ltd
Printed and bound in China by China Translation and Printing Services Ltd

ISBN 978 1 406 24051 1
16 15 14 13 12
10 9 8 7 6 5 4 3 2 1

British Library Cataloguing in Publication Data
McManus, Lori.
  Producing fruits. -- (The technology of farming)
  1. Fruit-culture--Juvenile literature.
  I. Title II. Series
  634-dc23
A full catalogue record for this book is available from the British Library.

Acknowledgements
We would like to thank the following for permission to reproduce photographs: Alamy: pp. 19 (© GFC Collection), 29 (© Global Warming Images), 32 (© Pierre BRYE), 35 (© jiashu xu); Getty Images: pp. 17 (SambaPhoto/Geyson Magno), 23 (SAID KHATIB/AFP), 24 (Hulton Archive), 27 (ROMEO GACAD/AFP), 41 (ROMEO GACAD/AFP); iStockphoto: p. 36 (© yungshu chao); Photolibrary: pp. 9 (Toshihiko Watanabe), 13 (FogStock LLC), 30 (Philippe Rocher), 31 (Stéphane OUZOUNOFF); Shutterstock: pp. 5 (© Margarita Borodina), 7 (© AnutkaT), 10 (© AJP), 14 (© Oleksii Sagitov), 15 (© Aaron Amat), 18 (© flypig), 21 (© Phillip Minnis), 25 (© Maresol), 33 (© Truyen Vu), 39 (© Gautier Willaume); © Vision Robotics Corporation: p. 42.

Cover photo of workers washing bananas reproduced with permission from Photolibrary (Imagesource).

Every effort has been made to contact copyright holders of any material reproduced in this book. Any omissions will be rectified in subsequent printings if notice is given to the publisher.

Contents

Some words appear in the text in bold, **like this**. You can find out what they mean by looking in the glossary.

What is fruit farming?

What is your favourite kind of fruit? It can be hard to choose among so many delicious varieties: juicy strawberries, sweet cherries, cool watermelon, crunchy apples, and fresh peaches. Fruit not only tastes good, but it also provides important vitamins and energy for the body.

Farmers all over the world grow the fruit we buy in markets and shops. Fruit farming requires knowledge about plants, careful attention to growing conditions, and **technology** to assist with the farming process. Some fruit farming methods are more helpful to people and the **environment** than others.

This diagram shows the life cycle of an apple tree.

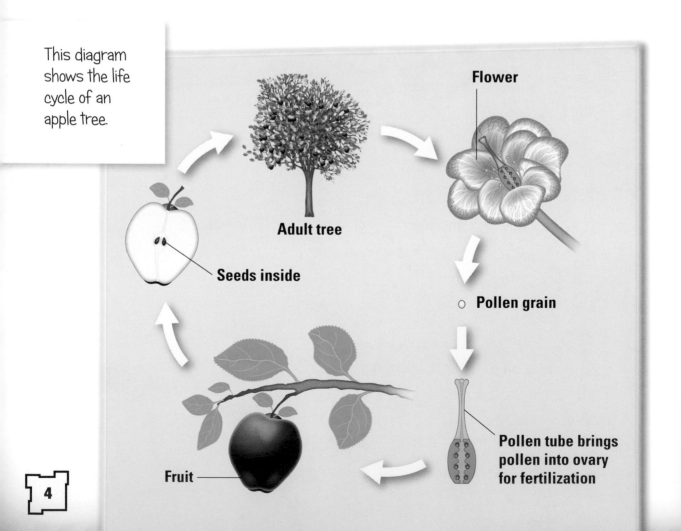

Flower

Adult tree

Seeds inside

○ **Pollen grain**

Pollen tube brings pollen into ovary for fertilization

Fruit

Unlike most fruits, the seeds of strawberries develop on the outside of the flesh rather than inside. Strawberries grow on low plants that send out **runners** to form new plants.

How does fruit grow?

Fruit grows naturally on some plants as part of the plant's **life cycle**. The fruit develops from a flower and contains the plant's seeds or stone. The plump **flesh** of the fruit protects the seeds so they can eventually become new plants. Most fruit-producing plants live longer than a year. For example, peach trees produce fruit for 8 to 20 years.

Some fruit grows on trees. Tree fruits include apples, pears, plums, apricots, oranges, and cherries. Some fruit grows on vines, such as grapes and melons. Blueberries and raspberries grow on bushes. Bananas grow on a tall plant that is considered to be a herb rather than a tree, because it does not have a trunk made of wood.

Where does fruit grow?

Fruit grows all over the world. But certain kinds of fruit grow best in specific **climates**. For example, pineapples grow best with warm weather all year and plenty of rain. The type of weather in a location helps a farmer determine what type of fruit **crop** to grow.

Fruit farms have different names depending on the type of fruit being grown. Fruit farms with trees planted in long rows are called orchards. Farms that grow grapes are called vineyards. Bananas are grown on farms called plantations.

Technology in fruit farming

Fruit farming began over 8,000 years ago. Since that time, farmers have used a variety of tools, equipment, and methods to help their fruit crops grow. Some tools, such as the **plough**, have been used for thousands of years. Other farming methods are very new, such as using robots to pick strawberries.

Today, fruit farmers have many choices of tools and methods. For example, farmers can use powerful chemicals to keep insects from ruining fruit crops. The chemicals work well, but they can have negative effects on the environment and people. Some farmers choose to release ladybirds instead. The ladybirds feed on the harmful insects.

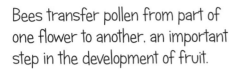

Bees transfer pollen from part of one flower to another, an important step in the development of fruit.

Bees

Farmers often use bees to **pollinate** fruit trees. The bees are released among the trees in spring when the flowers are open. In recent years, the wild bee population has decreased significantly due to diseases. Farmers use bees that have been reared by trained beekeepers.

When did fruit farming begin?

Fruit farming began between 6000 and 3000 BC. Ancient art, written records, and remains of fruit found at ancient locations have helped scientists determine these dates.

The beginning of agriculture

Before 10,000 BC, ancient people moved from place to place to find food. They hunted animals, caught fish, and collected fruit where it grew naturally. **Agriculture** began around 9500 BC, when people started raising animals and growing plants for food. Fruit farming started around 6000 BC with **crops** such as figs, plums, and grapes.

Evidence from the ancient world

Fruit farming began in the ancient **civilizations** of Mesopotamia and Egypt. In present-day Iran, scientists have found the remains of grapes inside clay pots dating back to 5000 BC. Egyptian tomb paintings from 1900 BC show monkeys helping farmers pick fruit from trees.

People in ancient India and China also grew fruit crops. Mangoes and oranges were farmed in these areas by 3000 BC. Bananas appear in wall paintings in India from around 450 BC. By 200 BC the ancient Chinese civilization had become wealthy from agriculture. Books from the Han dynasty in China (206 BC – AD 220) record information on protecting peach and mandarin orange trees from insects.

Figs were one of the first **cultivated** fruit crops. Fig trees grow about 9 metres (30 feet) high and produce two or three crops of fruit each year.

The plough

A **plough** is a tool that breaks up soil and prepares it for planting. Ploughs were invented in the Middle East soon after agriculture began. The earliest ploughs, called ards, were probably made from sharpened tree branches. They were pulled by two oxen so that the animals' strength could be used to turn the soil over. In the 1800s, factories began producing metal ploughs. After 1860, ploughs could be pulled by steam engines instead of animals. Today, metal ploughs are pulled behind tractors.

What about water?

Growing fruit trees and grapevines requires plenty of water. Ancient people invented **irrigation** systems to provide regular water for crops. The Mesopotamians built the first simple irrigation system around 7000 BC. The earliest large-scale irrigation system was created around 4000 BC in southern Russia. This system had **canals** up to 3 metres (10 feet) across and more than 1.6 kilometres (a mile) long!

Some farmers in poor countries still use ploughs pulled by animals.

By 2800 BC, the Egyptian government hired people specifically to build and supervise irrigation systems. Written records show the Egyptians built a 106-metre-long (350-foot-long) **dam** on the River Nile around 2500 BC to control the flow of water. Irrigation was being used in China by 2200 BC.

Farmers in ancient Greece built small dams across streams and brought up water from wells so they could grow fruit crops. In *The Odyssey*, written around 700 BC, the famous Greek poet Homer describes pear, pomegranate, apple, and fig trees growing well in Greece.

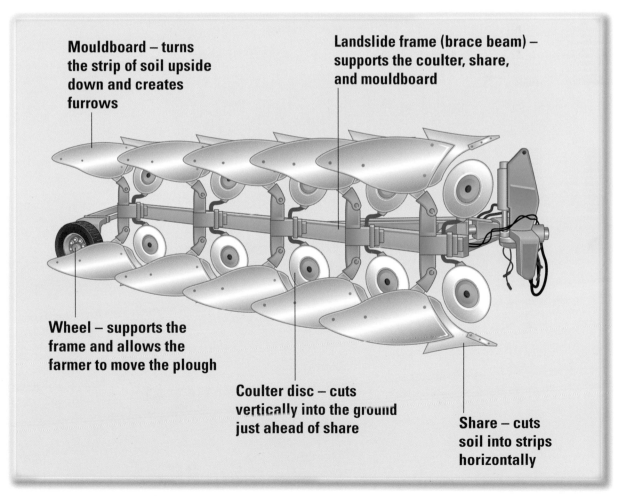

Mouldboard – turns the strip of soil upside down and creates furrows

Landslide frame (brace beam) – supports the coulter, share, and mouldboard

Wheel – supports the frame and allows the farmer to move the plough

Coulter disc – cuts vertically into the ground just ahead of share

Share – cuts soil into strips horizontally

Modern ploughs are lowered and raised hydraulically, using liquids under pressure.

How did fruit farming spread around the world?

Fruit farming spread as people travelled to different areas around the world. Countries sent individuals and armies to explore, conquer, and trade with other nations. The adventurers often brought fruit seeds and young plants back to their homelands. Farmers made changes to their land so that they could grow new types of fruit.

The Roman and Arab empires

In the Roman Republic (500–27 BC), grapes, apples, and plums were common **crops** around the Mediterranean Sea. As the Roman Empire (27 BC–AD 476) expanded, farmers planted new fruit crops such as cherries, apricots, and peaches introduced by travellers. Roman sea traders brought home young orange trees from India in around AD 100.

After AD 600, Arab armies began taking control of lands in North Africa, the Middle East, and Asia, creating an Arab Empire. Farming techniques and fruit crops spread to new areas. In AD 644, Arab scientists developed a windmill to pump water for **irrigation**. By AD 1000, Arabs introduced **fertilizers** to enrich farm soil. About this time, Arab traders introduced mango trees to North Africa.

Curved harvest knife

Knives have been used for thousands of years to cut **ripe** fruit off vines. Even today farmworkers use special curved knives to **harvest** grapes, strawberries, and melons such as cantaloupe and honeydew. Harvesting by hand prevents damage to the fruit. Also, many farmers cannot afford to buy expensive harvesting machines.

Farmworkers use curved knives to cut delicate grapes off the vines.

The age of exploration spreads fruit

From the early 1400s to the 1700s, ocean-going ships became stronger and safer. European countries sent citizens to explore and establish trading relationships with countries in Africa, Asia, South America, and the Caribbean. During this period, fruit seeds and plants travelled across oceans to new locations.

Brought over from the Caribbean, the pineapple became popular in Europe and Asia by the mid-1500s. Melons were introduced in Mexico and South America by Spanish explorers. The Spanish also brought peaches to Florida, where farming peaches became popular with American Indians. The practice of farming grapes spread from Europe to Africa, Australia, and the Americas between 1500 and 1800.

The US state of Georgia is known as the Peach State. However, peaches were actually brought to the United States by the Spanish.

Kiwi seeds were first introduced to New Zealand by Mary Isabel Fraser.

Changing the land

Not all fruit crops grew well if the new location was very different from the old one. Farmers often cleared trees or drained water from soggy areas to make planting crops possible. Soil was poured into low areas to flatten the land. Farmers sometimes built **greenhouses** or walls around gardens to grow warm-weather crops in colder **climates**.

Mary Isabel Fraser (1863–1942)

In the early 1900s, Mary Isabel Fraser visited China and tasted kiwi fruit for the first time. She brought kiwi fruit seeds back home to New Zealand. With the help of a gardener, Fraser grew the first New Zealand crop of kiwi fruits in 1910. Today, the country of New Zealand produces one-third of the world's supply of kiwi fruit.

Where are fruit farms located today?

Fruit farms can be found all over the world. The most successful **crops** are those that are best suited to the **climate** and the growing conditions of an area. Today, farmers can improve conditions through **irrigation**, **fertilizers**, and **cover crops**.

Tropical fruits

The **equator** is located in Earth's tropical climate zone. The tropical zone has warm weather with plenty of rain all year. Fruit such as pineapples, persimmons, papayas, and bananas grow best in this climate.

Bananas are the number-one fruit crop in the world. They grow in more than 100 countries on farms called plantations. India grows more bananas than any other country. The Philippines, China, and Ecuador are the next three top **producers** of bananas.

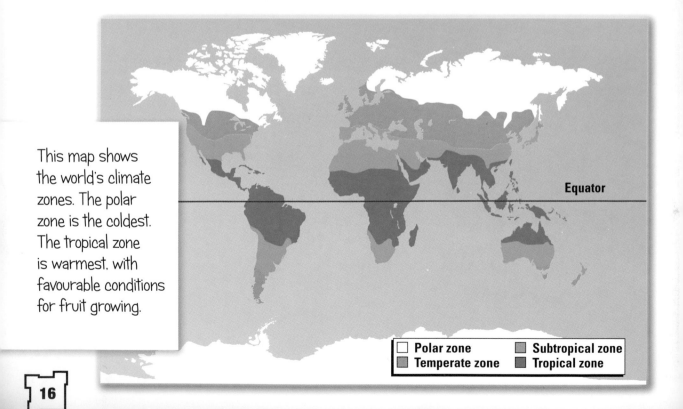

This map shows the world's climate zones. The polar zone is the coldest. The tropical zone is warmest, with favourable conditions for fruit growing.

Equator

☐ **Polar zone** ▨ **Subtropical zone**
▨ **Temperate zone** ▨ **Tropical zone**

Subtropical fruits

Some fruits grow best in the subtropical climate zone (see map). The subtropical zone has mild weather and typically does not experience frost during winter. Fruits that grow best in a subtropical climate include pomegranates, guava, lemons, and grapefruits. Oranges are the most widely grown subtropical fruit crop in the world. Brazil grows more oranges than any other country. The United States is the second-largest producer of oranges.

Harvest bins

When fruits are **harvested** by hand, they are immediately placed in plastic, cardboard, cloth, or woven bins. These bins are then transported to indoor locations. Often bins are rectangular so they can be stacked on top of one another. Some bins are so large they must be lifted by machine.

Farmworkers gently stack the fruit inside harvest bins. These bins can be lifted with two hands.

Temperate climate zone

Earth's temperate climate zone has weather that varies with the seasons. Summers are hot and winters are cold. Pears, peaches, apricots, plums, cherries, blueberries, and raspberries grow in the temperate zone.

Apples are also a common temperate fruit. More than 6,000 different kinds of apples are grown around the world. The biggest producer of apples is China. The United States, Iran, Turkey, Russia, Italy, and India also grow large crops of apples.

Strawberry farmers often cover the soil with plastic sheets to keep it moist. Holes are created to allow the strawberry plants to touch the air and grow upwards towards the Sun.

Water evaporates quickly from the large leaves of date palms. Farmers create irrigation systems to be sure date palms get enough water to grow sweet fruit.

Growing conditions

Why is a certain location selected for fruit farming? Besides climate, farmers also consider how the growing conditions will affect a particular fruit crop. These conditions include the type of soil and water supply in the area. Farmers also consider the **elevation**, the shape of the land, and the amount of time it will take to transport a delicate fruit to a market.

Farmers can improve the conditions of an area by using science-based tools. For example, strawberries grow best in **moist** soil. If the area does not get enough rain, farmers use irrigation lines to provide an ongoing supply of water. Many strawberry farmers also cover the soil with plastic so the water stays in the soil instead of **evaporating** into the air.

Caring for the soil

Fruit crops grow best in soil containing **nutrients**. If the soil lacks certain nutrients, a farmer will often apply a fertilizer. A farmer may also choose to grow a cover crop, such as beans or oats. Instead of using these plants as food for people, the farmer plows the cut crops into the soil. When the plants break down, they provide nutrients to the soil. Then the fruit can be grown in healthy soil.

If fruit crops are planted on hillsides or windy areas, farmers must prevent soil **erosion**. Often cover crops are grown around fruit trees to keep the soil in place. For example, a farmer may grow grass between orange trees grown on hills. Farmers may also plant tall, dense trees at the edges of a fruit farm. These trees provide a **windbreak**, which helps prevent soil erosion.

Tractors

Farmers use tractors to push and pull heavy loads. Tractors were invented in the 1880s to pull **ploughs** through fields. By the 1920s, the all-purpose, modern tractor had been developed. With different attachments, tractors can now be used for ploughing, planting, **cultivating**, mowing, harvesting, and moving soil or heavy equipment. Farmers who cannot afford tractors or have small fields still use animals to push and pull equipment.

Modern tractors have thick, oversized tyres
to help them to move over uneven ground.

What does it take to produce fruit crops?

Farmers work hard to produce fruit **crops** with specific flavours, sizes, and shapes. Crops must be planted, tended, and protected from animals and extreme weather. Farmers make decisions about how far apart and how tall to grow plants. They must also decide whether to use chemicals.

Propagating fruit crops

Fruit farmers rarely plant seeds in a field in order to grow new crops. Fruit crops are **propagated** in other ways. Some fruit-producing plants are grown from cuttings. Cuttings are sections of another plant that are cut off and planted in the soil. The cuttings then grow roots and eventually become fully developed plants. Fruit crops that grow well from cuttings include grapes and blueberries.

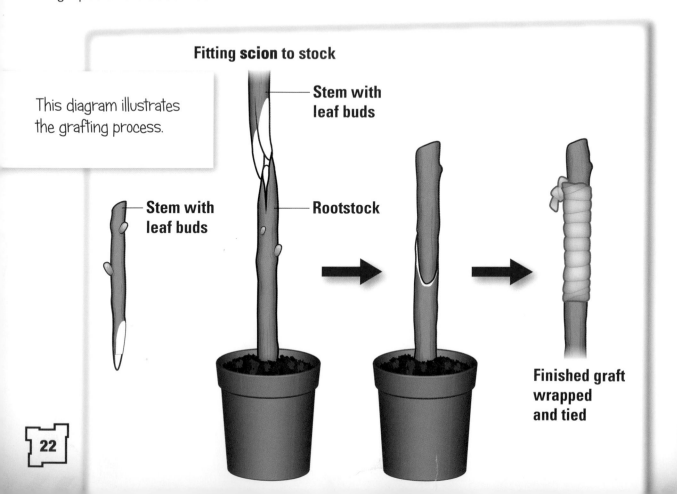

This diagram illustrates the grafting process.

Fitting scion to stock

Stem with leaf buds

Stem with leaf buds

Rootstock

Finished graft wrapped and tied

In a nursery, farmers carefully control the temperature, sunlight, water, and soil **nutrients**.

Many fruit trees do not grow strong roots easily. More often these trees are propagated by grafting (see diagram on page 22). Grafting involves inserting a stem with leaf buds into the rootstock (lower part of the trunk) of a young tree. Eventually, the stem becomes part of the tree and produces fruit. Grafting is used to propagate specific types of apples, pears, peaches, and other tree fruits.

Plants grown from cuttings or by grafting often spend one to two years in a **nursery** before being planted in a field. Young plants in a nursery receive special daily attention. Plants grown from **runners**, such as strawberries and raspberries, also spend time in nurseries before being planted in fields.

Just the right fruit

People and companies who buy fruit often want the fruit to have a certain appearance or taste. Farmers use **selective breeding** to propagate plants with the desired characteristics. For example, a farmer may graft new apple trees so that only apples with bright red skin are produced. Another farmer might choose to propagate only vines that grow seedless grapes.

Luther Burbank (1849–1926)

American Luther Burbank studied plants and plant cultivation. He developed more than 800 new plant varieties by using selective breeding and grafting. In 1893, Burbank published a book titled *New Creations in Fruit and Flowers*. In the book, he listed and described his best varieties.

Luther Burbank created new varieties of plums, pears, blackberries, raspberries, strawberries, cherries, apples, grapes, and nectarines.

Farming decisions

Many farming decisions affect fruit characteristics. Each farmer must decide how close together to place the individual plants in the field. Planting further apart means the crop will contain fewer trees and fewer fruits, but the fruits will be larger. Planting closer together produces smaller fruit on more trees.

The tallest, biggest trees or bushes do not always yield the most fruit. Controlling the height of plants helps produce more fruit in less space. Farmers may also change a tree's shape by cutting branches or forcing branches to grow in a certain direction. The shape of the tree affects its lifespan and the size of its fruit.

Apricot trees can be trained to grow against frames. The apricots receive more sunlight and produce plumper fruit when the trees are shaped like this.

Protecting fruit crops

Farmers actively protect their crops from danger. Some fruit will stop developing or die if the temperature gets too cold. Farmers may use metal heaters or small fires in their fields during cold spells to prevent frost. Other farmers may place fabric over the plants to keep heat around them.

Animals may try to eat the fruit while it is growing. Farmers often place fences or netting around crops to protect them from land animals such as deer and foxes. Birds can raid crops from the sky. Farmers use stuffed scarecrows, netting, and machines to keep birds away.

Diseases and insects can also damage fruit crops. Farmers take action against these dangers by using **pesticides**. Some pesticides are made from chemicals. Others are made from natural substances. Pesticides can also help kill weeds that a farmer does not want growing in the field. Weeds use up important soil nutrients and water needed for the fruit crop.

Crop spraying

In some countries aeroplanes are used as farm vehicles. Crop sprayers are planes that fly low to distribute **fertilizers** or pesticides on crops. Crop sprayers can spray large areas in a short time period. Some pilots use GPS (Global Positioning System) **technology** to plan their flight paths and record which crops have already been sprayed.

Crop-spraying planes have storage tanks and high-speed sprayers to distribute fertilizers or pesticides.

How are fruit crops harvested?

Many fruit **crops** are **harvested** by hand. Some machines can help with harvesting fruit. Farmers compare the cost of paying workers to the cost of buying and using machines. The size of the farm also makes a difference to how fruit is harvested. Farmers decide when to harvest based on the ripeness of the fruit.

Time to harvest

Most fruit crops are harvested when the fruit is **ripe**. A few fruits, such as bananas and pears, can be picked before they are ripe. These fruits ripen at the market or while stored. Other fruits, such as oranges and grapefruits, can stay on the tree for several months even after they ripen.

Farmers think about the journey of the fruit when timing the harvest. Will the fruit be at a market in less than a day? Will it be transported a long distance before being eaten? Fruits that will be eaten shortly after harvest are picked when they are quite ripe. Fruits are harvested as close as possible to the time of eating.

Cherry picker

A cherry picker is a platform or large, strong basket that can be raised into the air hydraulically. Pulled by a tractor or pushed by hand, the cherry picker is moved along rows of fruit trees. Cherry pickers help farmers harvest cherries as well as other tree fruits, such as peaches and oranges.

Standing on a cherry picker high off the ground, a farmworker can harvest fruits on trees with a knife or clippers.

Hand vs machine harvesting

Berries and vine fruits such as melons and grapes are typically harvested by hand. Farmworkers use special knives or clippers to cut the fruits off the plants. These fruits are harvested by hand to prevent damage to their skin and **flesh**. Grapes are sometimes shaken off the vine by a machine, especially if they are going to be used for juice or wine.

Peaches, plums, nectarines, and other soft fruits are harvested by hand because they would be ruined if they fell to the ground.

Typically only large farms use harvest shakers. Small farms usually harvest by hand, as the machines are very expensive.

Fruits on the same bush or vine can ripen at different rates. Hand-picking allows farmers to harvest only those fruits that are ripe. They leave the other fruits on the plant for a while longer.

Tree fruits are harvested in different ways. Many farmers harvest tree fruits by hand using ladders or a cherry picker and clippers. Farmers with large orchards may choose to use machines for harvesting even if some of the fruit is ruined. The time saved by using machines is worth the cost of the fruit that is lost.

Harvest shakers

Farmers sometimes use harvest shakers to detach fruits from trees, vines, or bushes. The machine grabs part of the plant and shakes it back and forth. Ripe fruit falls into cloth sheets or frames under the trees or vines. The fruit gets bruised and will spoil if it is not eaten or processed quickly into juice, pies, or other fruit products.

Thinking about the costs

Farmers and companies who own farms must think about the amount of money they spend on their crops. They compare this amount to the money they hope to receive from selling the fruit. In order to continue, the farmer or company must make more money than they spend.

The biggest cost in fruit farming is either labour (people who work on the farm) or machines. People cannot work as quickly as machines, but they damage less fruit when picking it. Then more of the fruit can be sold. Small farms often rely on people because they cannot afford machines. Large farms usually use machines. The initial cost is high, but the machines cut down the time for harvesting and the money spent on labour.

Pressing fruit too close together in a container can damage it. Farmers often choose packaging materials that prevent the fruits from touching each other.

From farm to market

Farmers and companies think about what will help their fruit crops to sell well at markets. Customers tend to buy fruit that looks good. Farmers use packaging materials such as trays and plastic bags to protect the fruit. Companies sometimes spray the fruit with special ingredients to make it appear shiny and smooth.

Camlin Fine Chemicals

Based in India, Camlin Fine Chemicals produces Nanofresh – a product for preserving fresh fruit. Made from natural ingredients, Nanofresh forms a coating on the skin of the fruit that keeps it fresh for longer without affecting its flavour or colour.

Nanofresh can be applied to a range of fruits to keep them fresh.

What methods make fruit farming sustainable?

Many scientists and farmers think about farming fruit in **sustainable** ways. Farmers can choose methods that improve their lives, protect the **environment**, and use **resources** carefully so fruit can be **cultivated** to feed people now and in the future.

Avoiding damage to the environment

Some methods of fruit farming negatively affect Earth's air and water. Air pollution increases when farmers spray **pesticides** on **crops**, use certain types of **fertilizers**, or plough their fields a lot. Instead, fruit farmers can choose to control pests in natural ways, such as using ladybirds. Farmers can also improve air quality by planting **windbreaks**.

Water quality is affected by farming practices. When water drains away from crops, it carries materials in the soil with it. If the soil contains chemicals from pesticides or fertilizers, those chemicals flow with the water. The water drains to streams, rivers, and lakes. The chemicals harm the plants and animals that live in the water.

Using more natural fertilizers and pesticides can prevent water pollution. Farmers can design **irrigation** systems and use **cover crops** to keep water in the soil of their fruit fields. Planting crops along the natural shape and **elevation** of the land also helps to slow down the run-off of water during rainstorms.

Ladybirds eat many of the insects that attack fruit. Farmers use them to control these pests.

Favorita Fruit Company

The Favorita Fruit Company is a leading banana and pineapple grower in Ecuador. The company not only grows and **exports** tropical fruit but also creates fertilizers and food packaging materials that avoid harm to the environment.

Some farmers in Kenya have recently starting growing passion fruit instead of corn. The passion fruit earns the farmers more money. A passion fruit orchard is shown here.

Soil for the future

Keeping soil healthy is an important part of sustainable fruit farming. Soil that erodes or loses **nutrients** each year will one day be unable to produce fruit crops. Farmers can plant cover crops to improve the nutrients in the soil, prevent **erosion**, and reduce weed growth. Cover crops can also help soil hold water.

Farmers may choose not to **till** the soil in order to improve its quality. "No-tillage" farming increases the amount of water and nutrients in the soil. Less ploughing also reduces labour, **fuel**, and machine costs. Farmers must manage no-tillage crops with special care. Otherwise, pest and disease problems can ruin the fruit.

Using land wisely

Farmers carefully consider how best to use their land. Some farmers choose to regularly change the type of crop they grow. This practice enhances soil nutrients and naturally stops some pests, weeds, and diseases. Some farmers choose to plant other crops in between their fruit trees. These farmers increase the amount of food produced and their **profit** from the land.

Herbert Bartz

Brazilian Herbert Bartz was the first farmer in South America to use no-tillage **technology**. Bartz investigated no-tillage farms in the United States and the UK, and he allowed experiments on his farm in 1971. Bartz has successfully raised no-tillage crops ever since.

Improving lives

To be sustainable, farming must improve the lives of the farmers and those in their community. Farmers need to make a profit in order to provide for their families and continue farming. They are more likely to make a profit if they grow several different kinds of crops on their land. Doing so reduces the risk of losing money if one crop does not grow well in a particular year.

Buying and selling food at local shops helps the community and the environment. If the farmer buys supplies at a nearby shop and sells his fruit to a local restaurant, the business owners and the farmer benefit. When fruit is transported far from the farm, the fuel used by lorries or aeroplanes releases harmful gases into the air. Reducing the distance food is transported also reduces air pollution.

Why not farm with sustainable methods?

Sustainable methods are practised by farmers in some areas, but not others. Farming companies in wealthy countries are sometimes more concerned about making a lot of money than protecting the environment. These companies continue to plough fields often and use chemical pesticides dropped from crop sprayers.

In poorer countries, many farmers are more concerned about their own family's hunger than improving the environment. They may not be educated about the most recent developments in sustainable farming.

Also, many developed countries demand fruit that is out of season or cannot be grown in their own countries. They **import** fruit from other countries thousands of miles away. This fruit is usually transported in ways that are harmful to the environment.

Some farmers in Thailand have learned how to regularly rotate crops in their fields. The farmers are benefitting from improved soil and reduced pest problems.

What will happen to fruit farming in the future?

Fruit farming has a history stretching back about 8,000 years. Although some methods have remained the same over time, farmers and scientists continue to improve and advance fruit-farming techniques. The near future may even include fruit-picking robots and vertical farms (see page 43) in unusual locations.

Steady advances in fruit farming

Scientists can already identify **genetic markers** in many fruits. For example, they know the sequence of genes that gives cherries a sweet flavour. This information helps farmers **propagate crops** with specific traits in a shorter period of time than ever before.

Some scientists take positive traits from other living things and introduce them to fruits. For example, scientists have discovered an arctic fish that produces a special substance to keep itself from freezing. By injecting this substance into strawberries, scientists hope to create fruits with built-in protection against cold weather. Farmers could then grow strawberries more successfully in areas that experience freezing temperatures during winter. However, most **genetically modified** (GM) foods have not yet been approved for sale in supermarkets. Tests need to clarify whether these foods will be healthy or harmful for humans.

Despite these advances in science, farmers in poorer countries continue to propagate crops in ways that have worked for thousands of years. Without large amounts of money or access to new information, these farmers use simple tools and hard work to produce fruit crops that provide money for their families.

Scientists continue to work on identifying genetic markers for desirable traits in many fruit crops.

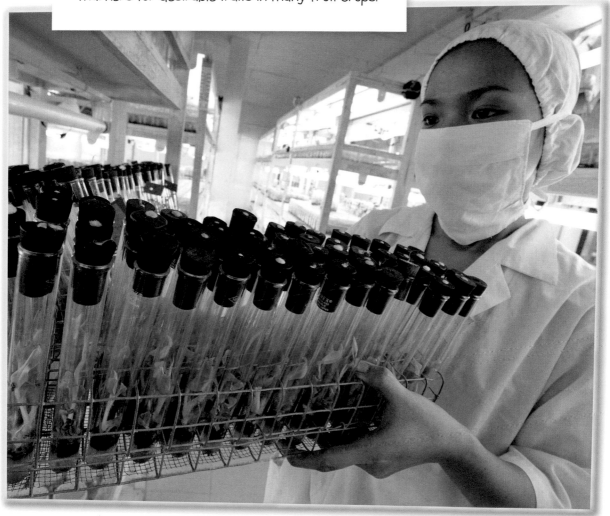

An illustration of a Vision Robotics fruit-picking robot is shown here.

Fruit-picking robots

A company called Vision Robotics is developing machines that can identify and harvest **ripe** fruit. The robots will move more slowly than humans because it takes them time to process information about the ripeness of each fruit. However, these robots will be able to work 24 hours per day without needing breaks, food, or water. In the end, the robots will pick more fruit in less time than people. Because the robots are expensive, only very large farm companies will be able to afford them.

Looking ahead

Fruit farming may look quite different in the future. Scientists are investigating how to provide **nutrients** to plants in other ways besides soil. Perhaps in the future, soil will not be needed to produce large fruit or vegetable crops.

Currently farmers and scientists are experimenting with vertical farms. These farms are built in skyscrapers that have many levels and glass windows on all the walls. Each floor of the building contains crops of fruit-bearing plants or vegetables. The farming company controls almost all growing conditions, including water, nutrients, temperature, wind, and even **erosion**. The vertical farms take up little space compared to traditional farms. They can be constructed in almost any **climate** or location, even in cities!

When you go to a supermarket in the future, ask the workers where and how the fruit was grown. You may find that the fruit comes from close by, or thousands of kilometres away. Who knows – soon the answer may even be "in a skyscraper".

Glossary

agriculture organized production of crops and animals for food; farming

canal human-made waterway

civilization highly developed human society

climate general weather conditions of an area

cover crop crop planted to provide nutrients to soil or to keep soil from eroding and weeds from growing

crop food obtained from the land at the end of a season of growth

cultivate to plant, tend, and harvest plants with work and skill

dam barrier built across a stream or river to block the flow of water

elevation height of something

environment external surroundings in which a plant or animal lives

erosion process by which the surface of Earth is worn away by water, wind, waves, etc.

equator imaginary circle around Earth equally distant from the north pole and south pole

evaporate to change from solid or liquid to gas

export to sell or ship to other countries

fertilizer substance added to soil to increase plant growth

flesh thick, soft part of a fruit or vegetable

fuel any substance burned as a source of heat or power, such as petrol

genetic marker recognizable trait, gene, or DNA section used for identification

genetically modified having to do with a living thing's genes that have been changed for the purpose of improving characteristics

greenhouse building with see-through walls and roof used to grow plants under controlled conditions

harvest to gather a ripe crop

import to buy and bring in from other countries

irrigation using artificial canals and ditches to supply land with water

life cycle stages of development for a living thing, from its beginning to the time it can produce young or new plants

moist slightly wet; damp

nursery place where young trees or plants are grown in controlled conditions

nutrient substance that provides nourishment

pesticide chemical used for killing pests, especially insects

plough agricultural tool used for cutting and turning over soil

pollinate to transfer pollen from the male part of the flower to the female part

producer person, country, or thing that grows or creates products

profit income or money gained

propagate to cause a living thing to multiply or reproduce

resource source of wealth in a country, such as precious metals, healthy soil, or oil

ripe mature and ready to be eaten

runner slender stem that arches to the ground and propagates by producing new roots and shoots

scion living part of a plant that is cut off and joined to another plant

selective breeding intentionally propagating plants with desired characteristics

sustainable capable of being maintained without using up natural resources or damaging the environment

technology application of scientific knowledge for practical purposes

till to plough land for the purpose of growing crops

windbreak line of trees, fencing, etc., serving as protection from the wind

Find out more

Books

Ancient Egypt (Food and Cooking In), Clive Gifford (Wayland, 2009)

Farming for the Future (Planet SOS), Gerry Bailey (Gareth Stevens Publishing, 2011)

Farming in the Future (Food and Farming), Ian Graham (Wayland, 2011)

Feeding the World (Food and Farming), Richard and Louise Spilsbury (Wayland, 2011)

Fruits (Eat Smart), Louise Spilsbury (Heinemann Library, 2010)

Fruits (Ingredients of a Balanced Diet), Rachel Eugster (Franklin Watts, 2010)

Websites

Eco-Friendly Kids

Visit this website to discover some tips on how you can become more eco-aware – and how you could grow your own fruit and veg!

www.ecofriendlykids.co.uk/FoodCategory.html

Apple Day

Started in 1990 by an organization called Common Ground to celebrate the British apple harvest, Apple Day has now become a regular autumn event in many towns and villages in the United Kingdom. Look on this website to find out about Apple Day activities near you.

www.england-in-particular.info/cg/appleday/a-events.html

Family Learning

Find out more about the importance of eating a balanced diet – and why this should include plenty of fruit and vegetables.

www.familylearning.org.uk/5-a-day.html

The British Beekeepers Association

Learn more about keeping bees, and the important part these amazing insects play in successful fruit and vegetable production.

www.bbka.org.uk/learn/bees_for_kids

Places to visit

Pick-Your-Own Farms in the United Kingdom

Pick your own strawberries, raspberries, apples, goosberries, currants, and many, many other types of fruits and vegetables. Visit this website to find out about pick-your-own farms near to where you live.

www.pickyourownfarms.org.uk

City Farms

Visit the City Farms website to find out about farms you can visit located in and around the city of London.

www.london.gov.uk/young-london/kids/things-to-do/farm.jsp#1

Whetstone Pastures Farm, Leicester

Enjoy a visit to Whetstone Pasture Farm and learn more about traditional and modern farming technology. You can also pick your own, or visit the farm shop for a variety of fresh fruits and vegetables.

www.whetstonepasturesfarm.com/farm-and-community.php

Index